The Entrepreneur's 90-Day Action Planner for Reinventing Life After 30

BUILT FOR MORE WORKBOOK

STEPHANIE WILLIAMS, MBA

Entrepreneur | Strategic Business Consultant | Real Estate Investor and Mentor

BOOKED & BRANDED PUBLISHING

The Entrepreneur's 90-Day Action Planner for Reinventing Life After 30

BUILT FOR MORE

WORKBOOK

STEPHANIE WILLIAMS, MBA

Entrepreneur | Strategic Business Consultant | Real Estate Investor and Mentor

BOOKED & BRANDED PUBLISHING

COPYRIGHT

Built for More: The Workbook – The Entrepreneur's 90-Day Action Planner for Reinventing Life After 30

Published by Booked & Branded Publishing
ISBN: 978-1-969369-15-5

DEDICATION

For every late starter who thought it was "too late" — this workbook is proof that your future is waiting on your action.

TABLE OF CONTENTS

TABLE OF CONTENTS

INTRODUCTION

How to Use This Workbook

This workbook is not meant to sit on a shelf. It's designed to be written in, filled out, and worked through over the next 90 days.

Here's how to use it:

1. One section per week.
2. Write it down.
3. Keep it messy.
4. Revisit often.

SECTION 1

Reset & Mindset

Exercise 1: Employee vs Entrepreneur Mindset Shift

VS

EMPLOYEE	ENTREPRENEUR

Exercise 2: Skills You've Been Giving Away for Free

Reflection Prompt: My "Built for More" Declaration

SECTION 2

Hustle Builder

Exercise 3: Brainstorm 10 Hustle Ideas

1. ____________________

2. ____________________

3. ____________________

4. ____________________

5. ____________________

6. ____________________

7. ____________________

8. ____________________

9. ____________________

10. ____________________

Worksheet: Narrowing to Your 30-Day Test Hustle

Action Plan: Launching with $200 or Less

SECTION 3

Platforms & Services

Worksheet: Matching Skills to Platforms

SKILLS	PLATFORMS

Exercise 4: Local Service Marketing Map

Worksheet: My First Client Profile

SECTION 4

Time & Accountability

- Exercise 5: 7-Day Time Audit
- Planner: Weekly "3 Money Moves" Tracker
- Accountability Contract: Partner Check-In Form

Exercise 5: 7-Day Time Audit

Set Real Deadlines: Put dates on everything. Don't just say, "I'll start marketing soon." Instead, commit: "By Thursday at 6 p.m., I will post my first ad." Deadlines transform intentions into action.

Day	Time Slot	Actual Activity	Ideal Activity	Comments/Reflection
Mon				
Tue				
Wed				
Thu				
Fri				
Sat				
Sun				

End of Week Reflection

Planner: Weekly "3 Money Moves" Tracker

MONTH:	WEEK OF:

MONDAY	TUESDAY	WEDNESDAY

THURSDAY	FRIDAY	SATURDAY

SUNDAY	NOTE

Accountability Contract: Partner Check-In Form

Write down who's supporting you on your journey and how they'll help you stay on track.

Partner's Name

Goals They Are Helping You With

List the goals your partner will help you stay accountable for...

Check-in Frequency

Weekly call, bi-weekly coffee catch-up, etc.

Notes / Expectations

Any expectations, ground rules, or reminders you want to note...

SECTION 5

Growth & Resilience

- Worksheet: Failure Journal
- Reflection Prompt: Positive Mindset Reset
- Tracker: My 90-Day Progress Grid

Worksheet: Failure Journal

Date _____ / _____ / _____

Mood Tracker

Choose a face 

Add a description ______________________________

____

____

Gratitude List

____

____

____

____

____

____

Highlights of the day

01 ______________________________

02 ______________________________

03 ______________________________

04 ______________________________

05 ______________________________

06 ______________________________

07 ______________________________

What I learned today

____

____

____

____

Goals for tomorrow

____

____

____

Reflection Prompt: Positive Mindset Reset

Tracker: My 90-Day Progress Grid

GOAL

MOTIVATION

PROGRESS BAR: ○ ○ ○ ○ ○ ○ ○ DATE COMPLETED:

ACTION PLAN

ROADBLOCKS

PROGRESS BAR: ○ ○ ○ ○ ○ ○ ○ DATE COMPLETED:

GOAL

MOTIVATION

PROGRESS BAR: ○ ○ ○ ○ ○ ○ ○ DATE COMPLETED:

NOTES:

CONCLUSION

One Year From Now

In 12 months, consistency will transform your hustle into income, and income into freedom.

Daily Affirmations & Journal Pages

My mood today: ☹ ☹ 😕 ☺ 😛 Date: ....

I am resourceful.

I am capable.

I am consistent.

Daily Notes:

WORK WITH ME

Your story has the power to create influence, income, and impact. If you're ready to turn your ideas into a professionally written, branded, and published book — I'd love to help.

At Booked and Branded Publishing, we specialize in:

- Ghostwriting premium books with speed and strategy
- Designing luxury-level workbooks and publishing packages
- Creating customized author branding and marketing assets

Visit

Website: www.bookedandbrandedpublishing.com

Email: hello@bookedandbrandedpublishing.com

to explore packages and book a consultation.

Let's build your legacy together.

Tagline: Where hustle meets strategy.

ABOUT THE AUTHOR

Stephanie Williams, MBA, is the founder and CEO of Booked & Branded Publishing, where she helps professionals, entrepreneurs, and thought leaders transform their ideas into powerful books, workbooks, and profitable brands.

After building her own business from the ground up, Stephanie committed to showing others — especially those in their 30s, 40s, and beyond — that it's never too late to build a life and business you love. Her straightforward, no-fluff approach empowers clients to see their worth, share their stories, and create lasting impact.

Through Booked & Branded, Stephanie has guided authors, coaches, and business owners in creating assets that not only share their voice but also generate income and legacy.

When she's not publishing or mentoring, Stephanie is busy brainstorming new ideas, uplifting entrepreneurs, and enjoying time with her family.

Connect: www.bookedandbrandedpublishing.com

Email: hello@bookedandbrandedpublishing.com

Made in the USA
Las Vegas, NV
03 November 2026

57420366R00019